Many Waters

Many Waters

Poems by

Evangeline Sanders

Cover design by Shay Culligan
Cover image from Unsplash
Author photo by Emily Free

ISBN: 979-8-90146-809-8
Library of Congress Control Number: 2026935134

Kelsay Books
502 South 1040 East, A-119
American Fork, Utah 84003
Kelsaybooks.com

For my family, with love.

Acknowledgments

Thank you to the following publications, in which initial versions of these poems first appeared:

Amethyst Review: "Offering"
Croak: "To the Froglet"
Delta Poetry Review: "Low Tide, Pawleys Island Creek," "Old Skin"
Littoral Magazine: "The Cave," "Boneyard Beach, Capers Island," "Black Horses," "Orion," "The Edge"
New College Review: "Four Clay Pots," "I stepped on a hickory nut, friend"

Thank you, also, to my professors and colleagues from the MFA Creative Writing program at the University of Alabama, without whom this collection would never have seen the light of day. Your thoughtful feedback has been invaluable.

Special thanks to Kwoya Fagin Maples, my thesis advisor, for her careful guidance and consistent faith in these words. I am also indebted to Joel Brouwer and Dr. Stephen Tedeschi, my professors and thesis committee members, who helped me generate and fine-tune many of these poems. And thank you to John Pursley III, my creative writing instructor from Clemson University, for his guidance and encouragement these past few years. Words cannot express my gratitude to my family. Without them, these poems would not be, and neither would I.

Finally—and most importantly—thank you to the Creator and Redeemer of Life, who casts out all anxiety and calls me into His presence, again and again, even when I kick and scream and run the other way.

Contents

III.

I.

The Cave

How hollow is this earth, how full
of want. Sweep of water, slop of sand,
click of crickets on shadowed walls,

muddy handprints on dimpled walls.
Time moves slowly, drips
onto our helmets, tickles our shins.

How strange it is to be here,
slicked with muck and ache.
Arm brushes arm mid-crawl and shivers

with words unsaid. Miles from the mouth
that teems with the world we know,
tempts with its sun-washed certainty.

We slip into these cracks
with the salamanders and bat carcasses,
in this hunched blackness, in these tunnels

that squeeze and press and digest,
in these hushed rooms with ceilings
that shimmer with droplets,

columns that grow with each drip.
This place is growing me, teaching me
to wait, to not see—to trip on loose rocks

and test for footing as we flick off our lights,
open our eyes to see a different sun
rising from the center of the earth.

To the Froglet

Gone are the days of who-you-were—
a flat brown whip, bulb-bodied,
flicking through algae and warm muck-water.
You are on the banks of who-you-will-be.
Gossamer tail and skin-flap gills
give way to budding lungs,
limp limbs that stiffen by the day.

The pond has shielded you
from turtles and ducks, the pink throats
that swallow new birth, but it is time
to shake off what is dead
and step into raw wind, open sky.

Your body may absorb your tail,
your lungs may swell and lead you
to land, but don't think
that transformation only happens once—
that all life is not shedding and sprouting,
a stumbling through the cold.

Breath

Here's what you know: the average adult breathes
twelve-to-twenty times per minute. Twelve-to-twenty
heaves of the chest, pumps of the lungs.
Humans can't breathe at the bottom of a sea or the top of a sky.
That's how scuba divers and astronauts die—
too much faith in aluminum tanks
and multi-layer polyester-nylon space suits.
You couldn't even snorkel in the Bahamas.
Who would trust a plastic tube and silicon mouthpiece?
You crave that full-bellied breath, that click at the tip of a yawn.
An assurance, a completion—a life well-breathed,
a breath well-lived. How could you settle for less?
Your blood oxygen level is 100%. You are so good
at breathing, at exchanging oxygen for carbon dioxide,
at making your chest go up and down.
You are so good at worrying that it won't.
And why? Why do you worry?
Your doctor says you should be grateful.
Some people have one lung and some people have half-lungs
and some people (like you) have two healthy pink lungs
like puffed-up Whoopie cushions.

Some people have punctured lungs and some people
have shriveled-up lungs and some people have lungs
for dinner. In certain parts of the world,
animal lungs and brains are deep-fried and seasoned
and sold in little packages. Sometimes you wish
you could sell your brain and purchase another.
Your friend says you should be grateful.
Phineas Gage had a metal rod driven through his brain.
Some people have half-brains and some people
have watery brains and some people
have brains with parasites and cancerous masses.
You wonder why your brain has annexed your lungs—
how breathing has become your life's obsession,
your bane and blood of existence.

Before Takeoff, Seat 18B

A passenger with a unicorn tattoo
watches a movie on his iPad
and sucks the sharp end of a candy cane.

In the movie, a woman screams as she gives birth
to a purple-faced baby. She laughs, cries,
cradles it in her arms. It looks like a frog,
all eyes and mouth and slime.

Are you aware that you're next to an emergency exit?
Yes ma'am, says the man. He folds his hands,
pleased to be chosen.

In the event of a water evacuation,
there would be sirens and orange life vests,
flailing arms, screaming babies. Then,
a wide, wild silence, blue arctic sky,
Big Dipper tipping onto our heads.

I would sit on the cold metal wing
and dangle my feet in the Atlantic and watch stars
blink on the black sea.

Worlds would dissolve and unfurl before me.
So much beauty, so much horror.

We will be taking off shortly.
Looks like it will be a very lovely night to be traveling.

Was it like that when the Titanic sank?
Everyone shivering in their lifeboats
on a lovely night, clutching their lovely pearls,
staring open-mouthed at a shattered dream.

Is there even enough wing space on this plane
for three hundred passengers?
Please sit back and enjoy the flight.

The man with the unicorn tattoo
watches a street stabbing on his iPad.
He burps and rewinds the scene, watches it again.
The plane starts moving and pivots into a sunset
and it is so lovely   I can barely breathe.

Low Tide, Pawleys Island Creek

Pockets of pluff mud suck our steps
as we sink up to our knees, smear handfuls
on our bellies, thighs, upper arms.

Y'all look like a couple of mud monsters,
Grandma calls from the sandbar.
She sits on the cooler in her white flip-flops

and dollar store tennis visor. Mother says *wash off,*
so we slip behind marsh grass and scrub
with salty fingers, submerging our heads,

burying our toes in shell-flecked sand.
An egret perches on tall twig-legs and twists
its neck, plunges its long, pointed beak into reeds.

Minnows peck our ankles as we splash
through rippling shallows and steer around oysters.
Fiddler crabs vanish into their holes, all at once.

When your grandad and I pass away,
Grandma says at sunset, *we want our ashes*
scattered in the Pawley's Island Creek.

That night, I dream someone sits by the oak
and dribbles ashes into the creek.
Black dots bob on the surface like water bugs.

A light wind stirs the pines. Fiddler crabs
salute with oversized claws.
An egret screeches and pivots its neck.

A hundred minnows halt mid-dance to surround
each speck of ash, whisper something
inaudible, sink into the dark green deep.

Boneyard Beach, Capers Island

It's how I remember it—petrified wood—
stripped trunks and stumps of oak, palmettos,

branches bleached with salt and arrowed sun,
sucked dry, sculpted into brittle arms.

Splayed roots suspended midair, dislodged
by a hurricane that slapped the shore in 1989.

Once, I chased my brother on this beach,
dodging high tide and light rain,

balancing on a half-buried palm trunk.
My right hand clutched a purple conch.

But this morning, fog hovers over trees.
Daddy straddles the boat and reels in

the rusted anchor. My brother watches clouds.
Mother shivers in her coat. Tomorrow,

I'll pack my suitcase, board the interstate
to Alabama, creak open a cold apartment,

stand with a blanket on my balcony
overlooking bare trees, a brown river.

I touch the branch of a dead oak
and picture the prophet Ezekiel, 3,000 years ago,

wandering through a parched valley,
wiping his brow, tripping over piles of bones:

Turning, turning, as a voice stirred the silence:
Son of man, can these bones live?

What Comes Before

medicinal white of pre-death // plastic syringe shoved into stiff rodent lips // squeals and twists of protest // death is not the nightmare // it's the moments before // bucking of a tiny body reaching for breath // stench of sour urine // you can't tell a guinea pig that it's about to die // that you're trying to swipe away the flies for a little longer // a little longer // trying to soak up every heartbeat // I've told people I fear death // I don't fear death // I fear what comes before // I once dove into the sea's glassy after-wave // sunk to the bottom // tucked myself into a ball // never known such silence // such stillness // thought I'd like to die this way when my time comes // wrapped in nothingness // nothing but my heartbeat in my ears // coaxing me to let go // no // I don't fear death // I fear the sagging eyes of loved ones // shoulders toppled with grief // coughs and pangs and staggered breaths // tubes wrapping around wrists // the drip-drip-drip of fluid bags // the way death never comes soon enough // the way it always comes before you're ready

Bubbles

A ten-year-old girl from Texas inhaled a brain-eating amoeba
while swimming in the Brazos River.
Her parents must have suspected nothing
when they zipped up the coolers
and tossed peach pits into the bushes
and cranked up the car. Only seven days later,
when their daughter fell limp, unconscious.
Nothing to do but watch
as doctors taped tubes to her face and friends
lined her sheets with stuffed animals.
How could they know until it was too late?
It happened so quickly. Like Becca,
who drove off the right side of the highway
and smashed her SUV into a tree.
She was wearing a seatbelt. She was there and then
she wasn't, like a fog of breath in December.
Did her best friend, Morgan, crumble on her back patio
when she heard the news? She had watched cancer
kill her father for years and years in a hospital bed.
Her mother called her during a field trip
in twelfth grade. *He's gone.* I put my hand
on her shoulder at Chick-fil-A.
I'm sorry, I said. She didn't even look at me.
I wonder which death carved the deepest—
whether grief is curbed or sharpened by expectation.
I wonder how some people get served death
on steaming platters while others haven't even tasted
its thick, charred skin. When I was five,

I was blowing bubbles with my brother
when I barged into the kitchen, started crying
for my mother. She dropped the wooden spoon,
asked what was wrong. I said I didn't want to die ever ever ever.
She grabbed my slimy soap bubble hands
like she was about to say something,
but she just hugged me. Even then, I knew
about empty consolations.

Fragments, Ireland

If you stand too long in a field of sheep,
you start to hallucinate sheep,
and sheep birthing sheep,
sheep in clouds and clouds in sheep.

*

Too many buskers on Grafton Street.
Too much graft on one strip of street. Enter:
woman with black cropped hair,
white fur coat. Boots that click on concrete.
I'll hand her a 10 euro note (that's the red one
with the stone arch, right?)
Slide me the tip jar. For her,
I'd wear it on my head, do a little jig.

*

Left side, left side. Left side passenger door.
Right, let's go. These roundabouts! Enter
on the left, stick to the left, left, left.
Dream of left so you don't forget.
Fold down sheets, brush teeth with dirty bristles,
left to right. Order Shepherd's Pie,
chew with left side molars.
No! I'm not driving, you are. Remember?
We already talked about this. Left, that's right.
Keep your eyes on the road.
Don't stare at sheep on rocks.

*

At the end of a rainbow,
there is a sheep, a pile of dead fish,
and fourteen shades of green.

*

Gaelic radio, station 4. Sounds like sounds,
tastes like rocks. Cold sky, 6. A.M. rain,
English Breakfast tea in a Styrofoam cup.
It tips in the cupholder, spills
onto the iPhone charger. Still too hot to sip.

*

These sheep are dirty.
Let's ship them back to the hostel,
throw them in the washer
with our jeans. Make them go bang-bang-bang
in the dryer. Scrape some crud out of their eyes.
They must be fresh and clean.
That's how it was in the beginning.

*

I’ve been mistaking English
for a foreign language.
Words slur in County Kerry.
Man with a red beard tells me
our table is ready. At least, I think he does,
but he may be speaking German.
I ask him to repeat himself.
He speaks louder German.

*

My brother gets so angry
when he’s hungry. That’s something
I’m learning about him. I’m learning a lot
about him. *Lighten up,*
I say. *We’re in Ireland. Don’t ruin this trip*
for us. I mean “me” when I say “us”
and he knows this. My mother used to call him
grump lump. I order Irish Stew
and he orders a pint of Guinness.

*

I'm throwing up today.
Must have picked up a bug on the plane.
I sip on a Sprite and we park our car
at a mossy overlook, alone
with the wind and rain and gray sea.
There's a cross and
cracked gravestone by the road. *Someone*
must have died here. We think it
but don't say it. I throw up again
on wet asphalt.

*

A man walks into a bar
and forgets who he is.
He remembers when the brandy
coats his throat
and a fiddle bow
slides across the strings.

Cliffs of Moher

Waters part for waters,
suck and spit, carve black rock

with whetted tongues. How much life
have you snared and swallowed whole,

you wild and unforgiving Atlantic,
you mouth of oblivion?

How many souls have wandered
these weathered cliffs in cold winds,

hugged their shivering arms
to their chest, stared past this grassy outcrop

to the shadow crouching
below, shimmering and expectant?

Sleep Paralysis

Chick-fil-A drive-thru register   monkey dressed like Santa
I'm wearing strawberry lotion   cash keep slipping   wet
hands   sore throat   mother drives me to a doctor's
appointment   seatbelt cuts my lap   I can't wake up
can't open my eyes   can't   move   the diagnosis   his
mustached voice   rustle of papers   I can't   wake up
ceiling fan hurls shadows   spins   everything   spins
wake up wake   up!   wooden library desk   swoop-
haired boy sits across from me   says I should remember him
seventh grade   I don't remember him   all I can think is
he looks like everyone I've ever known   blood stains my khaki

pants   Ms. Watson asks me to the whiteboard   boys giggle
from the back row   a guinea pig perches on my shoulder
opens his mouth   coughs up a rainbow streamer   I pull and
pull but can't see the end   it never ends   he is choking
dying   my friends return from their mission trips   bring
back suitcases   filled with dried-up worms   stick them to
a poster board   I wiggle my toes but   can't
seem to keep myself from tipping   off an iceberg into the
Arctic   all around I see bubbles   black-blue expanse
a ship snapping in two

To the Beaver

You uproot the land, your tail a plow
for mud, sticks, leaves. Life is a labor,
no time to rest, no time to prop up your feet
and watch water swell behind your wall.
Logs for today, logs for tomorrow, logs
stacked on logs to not run dry.
Building a home for yourself,
a heritage for your young,
a place to wallow in a world away.

You envy the spider's swift appendages,
the ants' sturdy backs, the water snake's
slither and twist. The salmon's grit,
its sleek body kicking through
rocks and currents. You have only teeth
and ambition, a slick-bellied waddle
as you drag wood across muddy banks.
You will not stop until your dam is the envy
of all, until every cedar topples at your feet.

Is life more than chiseled wood and toil?
The sparrows say you will wither away,
your teeth will crack and rot, the storm
will ruin your work and sweep you ashore,
but you chop-chop-chop, no rest,
and if the rains fell for forty days and forty nights,
you would beg to be left behind,
slapping your tail on this godforsaken water,
grasping at your pile of mud, sticks, leaves.

Terro

They stream from the L-shaped crack
in the bathroom wall—
a slow faucet drip—a new black speck

every half-second, spastic with desire,
colliding with oncoming traffic
in its haste to secure its share

of poison. They curse and honk
and grumble, flip some birds,
shake some fists, and suddenly

I'm overlooking Park Avenue
from a fourteenth-story apartment,
marveling at the chaos

of needing-to-be-somewhere.
They swarm the bead of poison
like elephants at a watering hole,

shoving for space, slurping up
every sticky drop, antennas twitching
with glee. Hauling in the borax,

bringing in the sheaves. *Praise the puddle!*
chants an army of starved, arthropodic bodies,
multiplying by the minute.

How bright is the road to illusion!
How sweet is the water that kills!

To Anxiety

You're obsessed with me.
You want to suffocate me in your arms
and shake my drooping shoulders
and bite my lips and never let me go.
You stalker, you psychopath, you rancid heap of vomit.
I ought to report you to the FBI. You make me sick.
You claw me till I'm limp as an armadillo carcass
on Interstate 59. You swoop in and scoop out my shell,
lick your dripping fingers. Go fling yourself into a ditch—
you're useless, you're worthless, you're selfish. I hate you.
Go jump into a radioactive sewage pond
and die. Jesus says we shouldn't hate our enemies—
that we should turn the other cheek,
so here, I'll give you my cheek: slap the life out of it,
slap it till its red and smudgy
and I'm huddled on my bedroom floor at 3am
sobbing into my knees. I can take it.
Give me the fight—the flash of knuckles,
the squelch of blood. You want some of this?
Everyone is so obsessed with acceptance,
but anger is the second stage of grief. Remember
what I've lost to you?
This is my poem. Get out of my poem.

II.

We Build a Lego Airplane

in the dark during a tropical storm,
my brother and I, criss-cross on his bedroom carpet,
our yellow dog in the doorway.
She and I are scared. My brother is not.
He hunches over the scattered pieces
in the glow of the headlamp, chin tucked
in concentration. Yellow on red on blue on green,
plastic slabs coaxed and snapped into order.
He tells me where to place each brick,
how to stagger them to angle the wings.
He orders, I obey, press pegs into holes.
Branches from the birch tree smack his window,
break off, tumble through the lawn.
Spurts of rain slap the glass, and I imagine my mother
watering the front yard, spraying the window
with her hose while we play in this room.
We always laugh when she does that.
We do not laugh now.
My mother watches the trees from the kitchen,
my father sits in his brown suede chair.
We bring them our finished airplane.
I'm scared, I say, and they fold their arms
around us. It is warm
and there is light in the creases of their elbows.
The wind screams and screams.

Orion

I don't care when a man dies in Omaha.
I don't care when a baby is born in a hospital
        5,000 miles away.

*

For years, I only knew Orion,

but I found him every time—a three-studded belt.
Something to grasp in a gape of sky.

*

A star dies every ten seconds.
It bloats red and collapses into a cold white core.
And then, a swell of blue light, a shrinking
        into blackness.

Orbiting planets grow cold and sick with radiation.
Some migrate, mourning a gravity.
The universe just blinks and shakes off the dust,
continues unfurling
        like an ever-blooming rose,
faster by the second.

The universe is like that—
what does it care? Every cosmic event
a shoulder shrug
in space and time. Old petals fall
        to feed the soil.

*

When Grandpa had his stroke,
he was just another eighty-year-old man
in the ICU
with a failing body.   But not to me.

*

I asked my father to set up our telescope
one night in December.
We pitched it on the sloped lawn
and watched Christmas lights blink on neighbors' roofs.

That night, no one cared
that I saw the moon's dimpled face
through a forty-dollar telescope,

that Venus came into focus
          with a twist of a father's hand,

that Orion perched stout-legged on our chimney,
that I was barefoot on cold grass
with a person that I loved

in some middle-class suburban neighborhood.

*

There's a peace
in being nothing
        to this world. In being
        a world. How strange
it is.

Poem for the River Birch

If I could, I would think about something
besides death and dust and acid sloshing in my belly.

If I could, I would write a poem about this river birch—
how my friend and I would rip off strips of bark
and fold them into scrolls.

How I'm pretty sure our neighbor
thought this tree was ugly
and wished it was on his property
so he could cut it down with his chainsaw.

How I didn't understand our neighbor,
or property,
or cutting down trees.

I would write about how this tree
would slough its leaves all at once,
and we would gather them together in November,

scatter them across the lawn
with our leaps and laughter.

How I did cartwheels in front of this tree.

How I cried in front of this tree.

How neighbors' mutts pooped in front of this tree.

How I saw moons and planets through a telescope
in front of this tree.

How the sun leaked through its gauzy leaves after a rain.

How the wind nearly toppled it over during a tropical storm,
and as its branches scraped the roof,
I saw the strength of roots, the stubbornness of soil.

If I could, I would write about these things,
and this would be my poem

for the river birch.

To the Dolphin

Bullet of joy and levity,
swift shot to the heart.
Smile, squeal, spin around
in your concrete tank. See the people
clap-clap-clap. Bump noses
with pudgy-cheeked children
through smudged glass,
coddle them with your clicks and clatter.
Be who they want you to be.

You are their smiles, their laughter,
their peanut butter fingers
that point and jab and tug at mothers' skirts.
Parents with video cameras:
Look, she's smiling! She loves you!
You don't know how to not perform,
how to not be theirs.

At night, it comes to you
in dreams: a vault of deep blue,
shafts of light.
A tail that carries you across a sea.

Reverie

Stillness and stones. An itch scratched
with each step into folds of river.

I'd run with the brown bears
in these woods, feral and bare boned.

Solitude like rawness in the belly.
Guttural howl to a half-moon.

Milky Way spilled above, snow
and wildfire. Each fill a salvation,

a raising of hands. Scuttle of squirrels
and moaning pines. A sky so big it aches.

Inheritance

2007

Grandma sheds her wig
in the yellow lamplight—
clump of silver wisps, cropped bangs,
splayed on the bathroom counter
beside the hand soap and toothpaste.

My grandmother, once furnished
like a full-foliaged tree,
spilling with curls and blossoms—

now bare, bald, peeled. A stranger
in a smudged mirror.

My mother says the doctors
pumped her veins with medicine
that killed her hair.
When I hear the word *cancer,*

I recoil, grow curious—pop it
into my mouth, suck on it
like a peppermint, spit it back out.

It tastes burnt, bitter.
It smells like chemicals.

2025

Sometimes I look at my breasts
and imagine a soft-lipped infant
drinking the light
and darkness inside me.

Sometimes I imagine
I'm in seventh grade science class

and my DNA is a clump of pipe cleaners
I can ravel and unravel,
ravel and unravel.

2018

The doctor carries a clipboard
with my genetic testing results.
Positive.

She shows me how to feel
for lumps in my breast

while my mother cries in the wooden chair
by the window.

It's okay, says the doctor.

It's okay, I say.
It's not your fault.

Pebbles

Blue-gray pebble snug in my palm—
flat and bean-shaped,
etched with cracks and mica.
I drop it in my pocket.

Guilt clings to unchosen pebbles,
the ones I see and step over.

Last summer, I drove to PetSmart
and chose a guinea pig with silky white fur,
another with a brown stripe down his face.
I left the third one behind,
hunched in the soiled bedding, head cocked.
Saw him again a week later, a black lump

pressed against a pink plastic igloo.
He didn't even stir when I tapped the walls
of the cage—when I said *I'm sorry,* turned away.
Guilt festers in finger smudges on glass.

I took a spelling test in first grade
and cheated on the word "pebble."
My teacher scribbled "100" by my name
in red pen, a smiley face with buckteeth.
I carried that guilt for weeks—
the guilt of what would have been
had I just taken the fall.

Maybe that teenager
wouldn't have tumbled from the mountain
that evening, maybe that dog
wouldn't have eaten those Reese's Pieces,
maybe that girl
wouldn't have scraped her knee on the playground.

One of the guinea pigs contracted a deadly virus
two days after adoption.
You can put him down, said the vet,
or commit to intensive at-home treatment
with no promise of recovery.

I remember how his body shook
when she wrapped him in a blanket
and carried him away.

Exodus

Let me ask you, Moses:

When God scooped the sea into His Palm—
sculpted it into walls, patted the land dry—

was the seabed like a cleaned-out carcass?
Were the Hebrews horror-choked

with visions of water tamed and trapped,
blacker than clotted blood, all that weight

of shadows pent up, ready to collapse
with the tap of a staff, a shift of a robe?

And when the waters sealed up behind you—
when you stepped, at last, onto rocky soil—

did you see them stuck to your sandal:
locusts, frogs, the blood of Egyptian men?

After you step on your guinea pig,

the emergency vet turns you away.
They don't accept rodents.

Tires screech on rain-slicked streets,
black sky with no stars, stoplights blaring
red-red-red. You drive him back home
because there's nothing else to do,
no doors to kick down in panic, no one to call
but your groaning mother.

She says you should have been more careful.

You know you'll be up all night
with your carelessness, his dying body.

You make a tent for him with your t-shirt,
stroke him in your lap, kiss his twitching nose,
feel his frail body shake beneath your hand.

Morning comes and there is no death.

Only life—still and expectant.
Second chance.

Black Horses

The photograph is creased at the edges,
wedged into a sleeved page
of my grandmother's scrapbook:
a little girl with legs like logs
half-tucked in sand.
Her mother squats behind her
in a floppy sun hat,
clutches a Tupperware
filled with watermelon chunks.
I hold the photo and I am there,
purple storm clouds
swelling on the horizon,
sweet bruise in the sky—

from my perch by the boardwalk,
the Atlantic looms like a herd
of black horses in the distance,
snarling and heavy-hooved,
slinging spittle from snouts.
My father and brother
bob on the dark swells, duck expertly
beneath each breaking wave,
reemerge in a pocket of fizzle.

How many hours do I kneel
with my pail and shovel in the hot,
white sand, sweat stuck
to my thighs, my father wishing
he could drag my dead-weight body
through the reeds and fling it,
head-first, into the waves?

Why don't you play with them?
my mother would ask
from her fold-up chair.
Why are you so afraid? I never knew
how to explain the black horses,
never imagined

that my time to join them
would slip in like high tide at midnight,
and I'd gallop into the fray,
all shins and spirit, to grab
my father's outstretched hand

as we faced the beasts
one by one.

I stepped on a hickory nut, friend,

and thought of a pond behind my childhood home,
green-scummed and swamped with mosquitoes,
white daisies scattered across the sloped shore.
And you, kneeling in a patch of clover and wild grass,
snapping stems, pressing petals into your palm.
When you stood, you held a hollowed-out hickory nut,
halved—*a little boat.* I knew it before you said it.

We stuffed two hickory halves with clover leaves
and parked them in our makeshift port.
Counting to three, we launched them into the open water,
watching our tiny vessels cut across the pond—
twin cargo ships, packed with sealed scrolls
and precious stones, destined for some sun-warmed shore.
You always rushed to greet them on the other side,
brown hair galloping across your back, stooped
over the shallows, waiting—breath clasped, arm extended—
to pluck them up and set them on dry ground.

I stepped on a hickory nut, friend,

and thought of a golden sky in November, when we stood
on those same muddy banks, stirred up ripples
with our toes. You held your daughter's hand
as the sun sucked the red of the horizon.

She has thick black hair, dark, almond-shaped eyes—
        she doesn't look like you, but I saw a sturdiness in her
toddling steps, a familiar fold of the brow
        as she picked up a hickory nut, examined the grooves
with her little finger. She was silent, unblinking, when she
        held it out to us, begged us to admire her treasure—
like there was nothing more precious than its gray-brown
        ordinarity, nothing more splendid than this strip of water
from which it washed ashore.

Dissection

I watched my first love
dissect a mackerel with a scalpel
from across the room. We were sixteen,
rolling fish lenses around in our palms,
pressing on gonads with gloved fingers,
sneaking peeks at each other
through smudged goggles.

For some months, I dissected my love—
poked his organs, tested his reflexes.
So, this is a fish. Stitched him back up
and tossed him into a wave.

When we broke up, my grandmother
rubbed my hand while I dragged my toe
through the sand. I didn't look at her—
only at the sea, swollen with wind and mud.
It just hurts so much.
I know, she said.
There will be many more fish.

And I've been trying to snag
a final specimen with my sharpened hook—
a fish who rises from the muck
to bear his breast to my blade—
a fish who digs his own heart out
and plops it into my palm—
the whole bloodied, dripping,
sweet-smelling mess. I'll know it for
the way it pulses, the way it fits
between my fingers.

I'll hand him my scalpel in return.

To the Swan

Emblem of love, skipping stones,
V-shaped wakes in velvety water.
Always beak-to-beak with another, heads bowed,
necks heart-bent towards the sun.
Where is your companion, little swan?
Why do you crouch alone by the willow?

The summer is gone and you are forgotten,
but you shake your wings
and cock your head and make yourself lovely.
This is your destiny. He is your destiny.
Maybe he'll come tomorrow,
maybe he came while you were asleep,
maybe he's stumbled into another's wings.
You watch the others glide through the lake
with their lovers—feather-boats—
light and supple as satin.

You can't leave your spot in the grass,
can't risk missing him when rises, dripping,
from the parted reeds to press his neck into yours.
So you wait—unmoving—
while the sun rises and sets, rises and sets.

Remember

When I enter my apartment,
my guinea pig rings his silver bell

and presses his nose
through the slats of the cage,
gnaws the paint off the metal.

When I let him out,
he latches onto my hand and bites
the bunched-up skin of my knuckle.

He's waited all day—wanted all day—
for the warmth of a hand cupping his head.

When I want, I am an empty-bellied ache,
rawness of a mountain stream.

When I want, I pace the hallway
and chew my nails and scavenge my phone
for notifications.

Sometimes I am a rodent
pressing a red button for a pellet.

Sometimes I am a gutted salmon
stripped to the bone.

Sometimes I forget about the birds
building a nest on my front door. Sometimes

I forget about the sound of a train
and distant thunder. Sometimes   I forget.

Dandelions

I pick a white seed from my hair at cruising altitude
and imagine I'm a dandelion, grinning
plump-cheeked in my patch of fertile soil.
I stretch to the sun like a stick of taffy.
Children snap my wet stem and blow my seeds
and spew wishes with pursed lips,
scatter them all over the hillside.

But have you not learned by now
that wishes are lies—fluffy seeds
that cling to the coats of unsuspecting children?

I'm telling myself a lie right now
to distract myself from this turbulence
(the lie is that I'm focused on dandelions,
not death-by-plane-crash). I close my eyes
and see a dandelion in an overgrown field
with brown and white cows, heaps of hay,
yellow daisies bowing by a stream.
A lady wrapped in a blanket grabs my hand
from across the aisle. I let go and smile my thanks,
wipe sweat, turn to the window to cry
at such strange kindness.
To hold the soggy hand of a stranger.

There is lightning on these dark clouds,
gold on black on gold.
The molecules collide in such a way
that I wonder how this world is so packed
with energy and beauty and lies
and strangers who would reach over an aisle
to squeeze my hand—dandelion seeds
that burrow and burrow in my hair.

To the Conch Shell

You've yearned to be unburied,
scraped with soft fingernails,
dipped in a breaking wave.
Water pink with sun and blood
that drips, drips, drips into your dents.
You're chipped, salt-drilled,
colder than these rocks and pines.
Worms have sucked holes in your skin,
roughened your spiraled neck
and peach-cream center.

Gone is the soft body inside you,
your days of slurping algae from the sea floor.
Are you more than a spiny husk,
a scroll of calcium—a memory
of an inhabitance?

I find you here at low tide.
I hold you to my ear and hear a sea
inside you. It sounds like an echo,
a strum of a storm, a hum-song of bubbles
rising from the deep. How long
have you been waiting in this patch of sand
for a hand to reach down, a sun
to uncover you? How long until you see
what lives within you?

III.

Four Clay Pots

I

The painting hung on the yellow wall
between two suede chairs
above the black TV stand.

My brother and I sprawled across
the speckled rug, shoving spoons
into chocolate pudding cups,
chatting and pointing to the painting—
the garden scene
inside the golden frame:

> Four clay pots
> against a brown stone background.
>
> Eucalyptus leaves clutter the border
> of the garden, coil around
> the mossy fountain, the crumbling statues.
> Tiny red berries
> dot the upper edges.

(We imagined popping them
into our mouths, puckering,
tasting the tart burst on our tongues.)

> *The first pot:* towering above
> the others, apple-shaped,
> two handles sticking out like ears,
> cracks sprouting from the rim.

(Our father, we thought, observing
the bulk of the body,
the hard-baked clay.)

The second pot: nestled in the shadow
of the first, slender,
puckered rim, ruffled
like a flowery blouse.

(Our mother, we thought, imagining her
gliding through the hallway
in her white skirt on Sunday mornings.)

The third pot: smaller still, chipped rim,
sturdy build. Hard, plain, boyish.

(My brother.)

The fourth pot: the smallest,
just a few swipes of the brush,
propped sleepily against
the third.

(Me.)

II

It hangs between two wooden cupboards
in the space above my new kitchen sink.
I scrub my plates with a dish brush
and stare at the acrylic garden,
ten inches from my nose,
eye-level. In the unfamiliar light

of morning, four clay pots
watch me pour orange dish soap, scrub, rinse,
pat plates dry with a hand towel.
Stretch, roll up my sleeves,
          repeat.

Elegy for a Siamese

In Memory of J.S.

When my mother drove you home
and draped you like a blanket
over my bony shoulder,
a purr bloomed in your belly.

After my first breakup, your ears twitched
as tears and snot dripped down
the smooth crown of your head.
You sat motionless, unblinking,
only springing for the door
when a can of chicken patê
popped open in the kitchen.

How many nights
have we slogged through the house at 1 AM,
grabbed old rags from the stack
above the washing machine
to scoop up your vomit, shake it into the toilet?

How many mornings have I awoke mid-dream
to hear the empty-stomached wail
of my Siamese king, rising like incense
from the foot of my bed?

Many nights ago,
when you crawled under my covers
and curled up beside my pillow,
pressed your body to my ribs,
I rolled over to face you. I saw you dreaming.
The grassland of your spine
slowed down my breathing
to match yours. Two pairs of lungs
sharing a beat as a round milk moon
peeked through the blinds.

Old Skin

She wades through the stream—mid-eighties—
pink brimmed straw hat, black and white one piece,

arms raised to her neck to fasten a tie. A shiver
and suck of air as she sinks into frigid water,

submerging the soft, white thighs, the pouty lower belly.
She floats on her back, eyes closed, fingers skimming

the skin of the water. Suspended in silence.
Streams of hair swirl around her pale, shriveled face.

And her husband, ten feet away, carving clear water,
kicking his stiff legs, grunting with each exhale.

When he finishes, he reaches for her tiny hand,
holds it as they step onto the pebbly shore.

Two wrinkled bodies stand in the sun and drip
on picnic blankets. They press white towels to their faces

to sop up shivers and wring water from limp hair.
Sheer skin, swirls of veins, dappled shoulders.

Old skin looks like a shell, a dried membrane.
A taut tarp stretched over bones,

sloughing off layers with each quickening year,
revealing the red-blue raw. Like when a bird

molts old feathers and shows what is gold and growing
beneath, shimmering like a stone.

Offering

Scan the shoreline, shuffle in and out of waves,
sift through shell fragments. Spot one
wrapped in a wad of purple kelp—a sand dollar—
whole, crisp, chalk white in a gray-brown array
of crushed conchs, chipped edges, holes and half cockles.
Trace the smooth, sloped surface with your finger.
See five slits surround five gray petals
with perfect radial symmetry. Imagine making an ornament—
soaking it in a bucket of bleach, slipping a ribbon
through the top slit—or slathering it with paint,
setting it on your bookshelf in a silver stand.
Stack several sand dollars in your palm and toss all but one
to the foaming waves. Watch the sea swallow, obliged.

Revelation Poem

No white horse, no thunder, no earthquake,
no voices like trumpets, no rushing waters,
no seven-sealed scroll, no six wings,
no sun like a sackcloth, no incense, no hurtling fire,
no smoking abyss, no blood moon,
no heavens rolling up like a scroll,
no wings like chariots, no great multitudes,
no silence in heaven, no white-washed robes,
no lambs standing, no ten horns and seven crowns,

just a woman scrubbing toilets in a Circle K,
two blue gloves and a bottle of Clorox spray,
black hair wadded into a baseball cap.
The sound of humming when I walk to the mirror
to wash my hands—a small, still smile that assures me
there is nothing she'd rather be doing
than handing me a paper towel
in a gas station bathroom on Christmas Eve.

Skellig Ring, Ireland

These sheep reek of muck.
Bellies smeared with dung,

strands of wool whipping
like barley in the wind.

When I enter the pasture,
they stop mid-chew
and tilt their heads, study me

like an oddity dropped
into their field—to think, a tourist!

Sneezing with each wet gust,
snapping pictures,

marveling at the lack
of her own species, the abundance
of another.

So many of them! Laughing,
laughing,
like she's never heard the bleating

of two hundred sheep
in the Irish countryside,

never stood on a cliff

and felt the salt-wind
slap her cheeks,

never seen an abandoned castle on a hill,
folds of green fields,

a rainbow
over a turquoise sea—

oh, sheep! If I lived among you,

I would herd you through hay
and half-eaten grass,
carry you over ditches
and mossy stone walls.

All the while, singing

to the clover and yellow daisies,
knowing they'd welcome
my warbly voice,

and I wouldn't even pluck them
from their patch of earth

because they'd look so happy
right there,

and I wouldn't even know of war
or what lies beyond this swollen sea,

and there would be rain
and more rain

falling in torrents,
feeding the roots and soil,

and all you sheep would lift
your black speckled faces
to the raindrops

and I would lie down beside you
on this muddy path

to cover myself with this wild,
wild sky.

The Edge

brown-green sling of muck   kelp   salt white crests
    spit of foam   slurp and gargle of churning water
waves splatter the base of the jetty   slap my feet   fizzle
        like soda   I can taste them
as they soak slabs of concrete   strike them   with a whip
fill the little holes and cracks
      with muddy water
grandpa once said   *jetties are constructed from a wide range*
   of materials: precast concrete   rocks   grout filled bags
the section by the shore   is light gray   dry as driftwood
  that's where   it's safe to climb
that's where   the white sand is a pillow
      to soften your fall
but here   on the edge of the world   it's slippery
  black with spray
daddy once said   *don't climb on the jetties   honey   you'll slip on the algae*
   split your skull like a shell
but here I am   daddy   do you see me?
        here I am   and I'm standing on the edge of a world
wind in my eyes   a pail of purple oysters
   by my bare feet
the moon is a pearl   I could pluck from the sky
        wipe clean
   turn over in my palm

Allotment

Giving birth in Spanish is *giving light.*
My twenty-four-year-old friend is pregnant with her third child.
She will feed him milk from her fertile mother-body
and burp his back and slather his head with baby shampoo,
scrub him till he's pink and sudsy and dreaming
of rubber ducks with little cowboy hats
line dancing to "I'm a Little Teapot"
with Squishy-Purple-Octopus and Smiley-Red-Crab.
She will buy him colorful teething rings and organic carrot puree
to satisfy his growing nutritional needs,
and then she will cry as he rides to college in his red truck.
Or something like that. I'm told how beautiful it is
to be full of milk, swollen with *coos* and sleep deprivation.
All my pregnancy dreams have been nightmares.
Is this concerning? My belly deflates or expands and bursts
into a pile of blood and pus. I don't know how to cradle a baby,
but I know how to hold a potato-shaped rodent.
I have a guinea pig who expels over a hundred poops a day.
I feed him chunks of yellow bell pepper to prevent scurvy
and bathe him in *coos* and clip his nails.

Every morning, I fill his bowl with pellets from my refrigerator.
Every evening, I sing him to sleep
and run my finger down his spine to hear him purr.
I marvel at my allotment.
I, too, give light.

will remain. I live a life lacking in abandon, abundant in remain. I have never been abandoned, have never heard the rattle of pots on the porch as the front door slams shut. I saw this in movies—wondered why there were so many stories about abandon and so few about remain. My mother once said "you're mine" in the pink glow of the butterfly nightlight. It made me feel warm and safe and confined. I was a red-faced baby pulled from her womb, pulled from her cells and blood, pushing her patience with every stiff-armed tantrum and panic attack. I know it wasn't easy. I wonder what it means to be a mother—to donate your body to a blueberry in the womb, all brown hair and brown eyes and anxiety and full-cheeked smile. Everyone always says I'm blessed to still have a mother and father. I know this. I know this when they sit me down and beg me to come back home. When I assure them that, wherever I go, theirs I will remain.

To the Loggerhead

Home is stitched inside you,
these dunes and sea oats that sway
with a warm September wind.
You cannot know why you returned
at midnight to the shore
that bore your first breath.
You cannot know why it creaks
in your bones like an ancient pine, why

some mysteries can only be felt.
Even tides heed the tug of the moon,
rise and recede, rise and recede.
You've seen seas unbound,
mountains and cliffs and caves
you still visit in dreams,
but it is here that you always emerge,
dripping, to swaddle yourself in
Carolina sand.

Future Husband and I

He says I can't eat spaghetti with a spoon. I eat spaghetti with a spoon to show him he's wrong.

He's always wrong. I'm always right.

He has reddish-gold hair that curls under his baseball cap, or brown hair that spikes gently in the front, or dirty-blonde hippie hair that brushes his shoulders, or black hair that clings to his scalp. I have thin brown hair that frizzes in the rain.

He is strong. I am getting stronger.

He is kind. I am getting kinder.

He cries. I love that he cries.

He plays the guitar, or the piano, or the violin, or the electric bass, or the ukelele, or the xylophone, or the harpsichord, or the harmonica, or the cowbells, or the triangle, or the digeridoo, or the Russian bassoon, or nothing at all. I play the mandolin.

He holds my hand when we walk on the beach and barge through the breakers. I hold his hand when he sings in the front seat of his SUV, or Jeep, or van, or truck, or sedan, or convertible, or golf cart, or (God forbid) tractor.

He always dreamt of meeting a woman with yellow hair and a modeling portfolio. I am not that woman.

I always dreamt of meeting a scientist with black-frame glasses and a monkey assistant. He is not that man.

He says, “Marry me.” I say “yes.”

He writes our life. I write our poetry.

When I die,

don’t scatter me in the ocean or creek
or whatever, cause I don’t know about you,
but I don’t want my particles getting all up
in some geezer’s personal space.
No, I don’t want to be scattered.
I want to lounge in the plushy ground
in a nice little hand-crafted coffin
with elaborate carvings of pomegranates and guinea pigs.
I want to have a nice little grave neighbor,
preferably the baseball-player-boy-next-door type,
with big tan arms and reddish-brown hair
and freckles and a tidy grin. I’ll call him Charlie,
and he’s very sensitive, died by blunt-force trauma
while crossing the street to deliver his Gram Gram’s groceries.
He always bags the frozen items separately
at the self-checkout, never leaves his towels
on the bathroom floor. And you’d better make sure
my hair’s not doing that flat thing that it does
when I’ve been lying down for a long time.
Fluff it up, do whatever you need to do.
If my mother’s still alive, she’s gonna try
to get me in some hideous puff-sleeved thing—
tell her I gave you permission to donate it to Good Will.

If I'm gonna be dead, might as well serve.
The southern ladies will *wooooo weeee,*
peek into the casket and say: *She may be dead, Laudie,*
but she's still got it!

Reflections, 30,000 Feet Above Girlhood

You leave Alabama with something sweet and warm nestled in your palm. You know this is confidence—a white lily on a dark blue lake, supple and open-armed. You look out the airplane window and see stars, clouds, clovers of highway. A city of gold stretched out like a sheet. Soft eyes and cold-cracked lips. You want to reach into your reflection for a little girl's hand and tell her to wait and see. Wait and see. See how you still get scared on airplanes. See how you still choose the strawberry sprinkle donuts. See how your future spills open like a pomegranate. See how you tuck your hair behind your ear and smile. See how a woman becomes.

Many Waters

waters that suck & spit
waters that shriek
waters that wage war
waters that slap black rock
waters that roll & swell & mix
waters that stack on waters
waters that carve out cliffs
waters that clog & choke
waters that kill
waters that leave alive
waters that chew & swallow & vomit back up
waters that bury the dead
waters that part for the living
waters that harden into ice
waters that crouch beneath waters
waters that hold shadows
waters that heat & crack & quiver awake
waters that drip from ferns
waters that spill over stones
waters that tip over heads
waters that simmer in caves
waters that watch & blink
waters that listen
waters that wait

About the Author

Evangeline Sanders is a poet from Charleston, South Carolina. She received her MFA from the University of Alabama, where she taught English classes and served as an assistant editor for the *Black Warrior Review.* Her debut chapbook, *Flight of the Quetzal,* was published by Finishing Line Press in 2023. Her poetry has appeared in various literary journals, including *Delta Poetry Review, Sky Island Journal,* and *Littoral Magazine*. Currently, she lives in Columbia, South Carolina and teaches first-year writing at the University of South Carolina.

www.ingramcontent.com/pod-product-compliance
Lightning Source LLC
LaVergne TN
LVHW010629100826
845148LV00014B/3171

* 9 7 9 8 9 0 1 4 6 8 0 9 8 *